EXPLORING

WASHINGTON'S

MAJESTIC STATE CAPITOL

THE
DONNING COMPANY
PUBLISHERS

EXPLORING

WASHINGTON'S

MAJESTIC STATE CAPITOL

BY CATHLEEN NORMAN

Capitol Furnishings Preservation Committee

OPPOSITE: LEGISLATIVE BUILDING CONSTRUCTION, OCTOBER 17, 1924. *State Library Photo Collection, 1851–1990 (SLPC), Washington State Archives (WSA)*

The Donning Company Publishers
184 Business Park Drive, Suite 206
Virginia Beach, VA 23462

Steve Mull, General Manager
Barbara Buchanan, Office Manager
Heather L. Floyd, Editor
Jennifer Penaflor, Graphic Designer
Priscilla Odango, Imaging Artist
Katie Gardner, Project Research Coordinator
Tonya Washam, Marketing Specialist
Pamela Engelhard, Marketing Advisor

Cathleen Norman, Project Director

Library of Congress Cataloging-in-Publication Data

Norman, Cathleen M.
 Exploring Washington's Majestic State Capitol / By Cathleen Norman.
    pages cm
 ISBN 978-1-57864-782-8 (softcover : alk. paper)
 1. Washington State Capitol (Olympia, Wash.) 2. Olympia (Wash.)--Buildings, structures, etc. I. Title.
 NA4412.W2N67 2012
 725'.110979779--dc23

                         2012032994

Printed in the United States of America at Walsworth Publishing Company

TABLE OF CONTENTS

6   A MESSAGE FROM THE GOVERNOR

8   ACKNOWLEDGMENTS

9   WHY FURNISHINGS MATTER

10   **CHAPTER ONE** Olympia—A Beautiful and Impressive Capital City

15   **CHAPTER TWO** Territorial and State Capitol Buildings

22   **CHAPTER THREE** Intervening Events

24   **CHAPTER FOUR** Capitol Group—Planning, Design, and Construction

40   **CHAPTER FIVE** Inside the Legislative Building

54   **CHAPTER SIX** The Capitol Grounds

61   **CHAPTER SEVEN** Earthquakes and Repairs, Preservation and Conservation

63   A MESSAGE FROM THE LIEUTENANT GOVERNOR

A MESSAGE FROM THE GOVERNOR

Welcome to the Washington State Capitol.

It is an honor to introduce you to our scenic Capitol campus, featuring our magnificent, domed Legislative Building, the Temple of Justice, and adjacent government buildings, as well as the Tivoli Fountain and the many stunning gardens, lawns, and monuments that so beautifully and artfully complete the campus. Washington's Capitol is a historic and architectural treasure, and we believe it is the most beautiful capitol in the nation.

We invite you to come explore our buildings, furnishings, and grounds and experience the essence of our state's impassioned citizenry and creative legacy.

Chris Gregoire

Chris Gregoire
Governor of Washington
2005–2013

Office of the Governor

EXTERIOR OF THE LEGISLATIVE BUILDING. *Department of Enterprise Services (DES)*

ACKNOWLEDGMENTS

Lead Sponsors:

Washington State Employees Credit Union

Olympia Federal Savings

Washington State Historical Society

Verizon Foundation

Steve Lindstrom and Sue Ponsteen

Peter and Jackie White

TwinStar Credit Union

Special thanks to:

Washington State Archives

Washington State Senate and Washington State House of Representatives

Washington State Department of Enterprise Services

Author: Cathleen Norman with the Capitol Furnishings Preservation Committee
Cover credit: Far Sighted Images, Photography by W. D. "Nate" Naismith
Title page credit: Washington State Senate

Other photographic credits:

DES		Department of Enterprise Services
WSHOR		Washington State House of Representatives
TPL		Tacoma Public Library
UWSC		University of Washington Special Collections
	HWPC	Harry White Photograph Collection
WSHS		Washington State Historical Society
WSA		Washington State Archives
	SPPC	Susan Parish Photograph Collection, 1889–1990
	SLPC	State Library Photograph Collection, 1851–1990
	GSPC	General Subjects Photograph Collection, 1845–2005
WSS		Washington State Senate

WHY FURNISHINGS MATTER

The Capitol Furnishings Preservation Committee was formed in 1999 by the State Legislature "to promote and encourage the recovery and preservation of the original and historic furnishings of the state capitol group" as envisioned by architects Walter Wilder and Harry White. The Capitol Group, according to state statute, includes the Legislative Building, Insurance Building, Temple of Justice, John A. Cherberg Building, John L. O'Brien Building, and Irving Newhouse Building. The Committee presents this publication to encourage the appreciation of the Capitol buildings and their historic furnishings as a legacy to the people of Washington.

Why do furnishings matter? So often, historic places are for looking and not for touching. Here in the historic spaces of the Washington State Capitol Group, however, history is still in the making and uniquely accessible to all.

STUDENTS, PARENTS, AND TEACHERS WITH REPRESENTATIVE JAN ANGEL IN THE STATE RECEPTION ROOM. *Washington State House of Representatives (WSHOR)*

In 1926, the State needed to purchase furnishings suitable for the monumental scale and quality of the nearly completed Capitol Building. Architects Wilder and White gave particular attention to this task. They developed detailed specifications for custom design and construction of furniture for the building's ceremonial spaces, chambers, and executive offices. Nearly all of these original furnishings are still in use in the building today, a testament to the architects' good judgment in choosing styles well matched to the grandeur, dignity, and permanence of the Capitol Building. Those who work in and visit the building can immediately experience the beauty and quality of these historic furnishings and use them on a daily basis.

This ability to share a historic experience—as when our governor sits down to work at the desk used by previous governors or when visiting schoolchildren sit in the velvet couches of the State Reception Room—inspires an understanding. It communicates that what we do in this building, the work of democratic governance, is a part of a continuum. We are invited to consider our place and our responsibility within it.

Historic furnishings have the power to impart a sense of continuity with the past alongside a tangible sense of time and progress. We see, touch, and feel what has changed over time, and, equally important, what has not. As past and present come together, we can literally take our seat in history.

CHAPTER ONE

OLYMPIA—A BEAUTIFUL AND IMPRESSIVE CAPITAL CITY

Located at the southernmost tip of Puget Sound, Olympia enjoys views of its distant namesake mountains and the snowy slopes of Mount Rainier. Sustained by government, wood processing, commerce, and shipping, it has been Washington's capital city since the Washington Territory was created in 1853, oftentimes fiercely fighting to keep the privilege.

South Puget Sound Coastal Salish people first resided in what is now Olympia. The ancestors of the present-day Squaxin Island Tribe lived in one or more permanent villages in Olympia for perhaps thousands of years before Euro-American settlement. They named the place bəsčətxʷəd, meaning "a place that has bears." The people of this village were known as Steh-Chass.

Americans settled in Olympia in the 1840s, where New Englander Edmund Sylvester platted the town site (including donated land for the present Capitol grounds) in 1850, naming it for the majestic view of the Olympic Mountains. Two years later, Olympia became the county seat of the newly created Thurston County, still a part of Oregon Territory.

"Northern Oregonians" residing north of the Columbia River soon felt their interests were under-represented by the territorial legislature in faraway Salem. A rousing speech by Olympia lawyer Daniel Bigelow on July 4, 1852, further stirred the movement to create a new territory north of the river. The Northern Oregonians appealed to the U.S. Congress to form a separate territory called "Columbia." President Millard Fillmore signed legislation on March 2, 1853, creating "Washington Territory," named to honor the nation's first president.

Isaac Ingalls Stevens was appointed governor of the new territory that extended east from the Pacific Ocean into the mountainous area that would become northern Idaho and western Montana. He arrived in Olympia in November 1853 to find muddy streets, scattered stumps, and an assortment of wooden buildings.

VOTE OLYMPIA FOR THE CAPITAL, 1889. *Washington State Historical Society (WSHS), EPH-B979.7791/V941v/1889*

OPPOSITE: PAINTING, OIL ON CANVAS, OLYMPIA, WASHINGTON TERRITORY, CA. 1872 BY ELIZABETH O. KIMBALL. *WSHS, C1943.15x.5*

Stevens likely chose Olympia as the site of the first legislative assembly because it already had a customs office, post office, and the territory's first newspaper, *The Columbian*. With 996 residents, Thurston was the most populous county on Puget Sound.

Named the permanent Territorial Capital in 1855, the city developed along the waterfront as a hub of maritime commerce, incorporating in 1859. All the while, Olympians catered to the legislators, intent on making their town Washington's permanent capital city. Over the years, Olympia fended off several challenges from other cities to relocate the capital. Vancouver, North Yakima, Tacoma, Ellensburg, Steilacoom, Seattle, and Port Townsend each vied to become the capital city at one time or another.

On November 11, 1889, Washington became the forty-second state to enter the Union, and Olympia became the State Capital, confirmed by an 1890 statewide vote.

With the Capitol building located downtown in the early 1900s, the city enjoyed a period of prosperity and rebuilt many of the wooden storefronts into more modern business blocks of brick, stone, stucco, and concrete, which lend historic ambience to the city today.

Progress and prosperity continued in the early twentieth century. The women of Washington campaigned and won the right to vote in 1910, the fifth state in the Union to permanently secure women's suffrage. The city expanded in 1911–1912 when over twenty blocks were created by a massive project that dredged a deepwater harbor and filled the sloughs north and east of downtown. New enterprises began operation on the fill, including shipbuilding during World War I and the Port

INAUGURATION OF FIRST STATE GOVERNOR ELISHA P. FERRY, NOVEMBER 18, 1889. *Photo by A. D. Rogers, Inauguration of Governor Ferry Photographs, 1889, Washington State Archives (WSA)*

CAPITOL WAY, CA. 1940S. *Ellis Postcard, Private Collection*

OLYMPIA MAIN STREET (NOW CAPITOL WAY) LOOKING SOUTH, CA. 1890. *WSHS, C1952.284.11*

of Olympia formed in 1922 to ship products from nearby industries. From the 1910s through the 1930s, Capitol Group construction employed hundreds and transformed the city.

As elsewhere in the country, Olympia's economy sputtered, then stalled during the Great Depression of the 1930s. Federal works projects assisted the unemployed and helped construct several of the current Capitol campus buildings.

Interstate 5, built in the 1950s, came through the city in a sweeping arc close to the Capitol and downtown, giving travelers a spectacular view of the Legislative Building dome. The Deschutes River, dammed in 1951, created Capitol Lake, a reflecting pool for the Capitol Group.

Seeing state agency headquarters going to other cities, a group of Olympia citizens sued and won a court case to return all of the headquarters to the capital city in 1954. The Capitol campus expanded to the north and east of the historic Capitol Group with new office buildings in modern designs to accommodate the larger state population and growing government presence in the city.

As old industries gave way, new buildings and activities filled portions of the waterfront and downtown in the 1980s and 1990s, including a farmer's market and community and

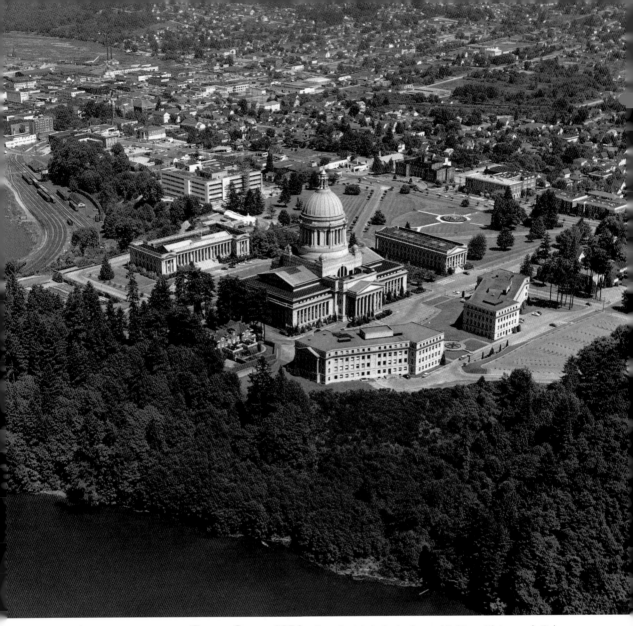

AN AERIAL VIEW OF THE CAPITOL GROUP, 1956. *Photo by Merle Junk, General Subjects Photograph Collection, 1845–2005 (GSPC), WSA*

cultural centers. Heritage Park, a new feature for the Capitol campus in 2003, provides northward expansion of the traditional Capitol grounds with a well-used public greenway around Capitol Lake. Part of the original Olmsted landscape concept for the Capitol grounds, the esplanade park was finally achieved in the early twenty-first century, connecting the campus and lake with the downtown core.

Through continued preservation and care by the state, the Capitol Group continues to provide an impressive backdrop for the historic city of Olympia and its signature waterfront.

CHAPTER TWO

TERRITORIAL AND STATE CAPITOL BUILDINGS

EIGHT-DAY WALL CLOCK USED CA. 1854 IN THE PARKER & COLTER BUILDING IN THE LEGISLATIVE CHAMBERS. *WSHS, C1943.1038.1*

TOP: THE ORIGINAL MEETING SITE OF THE WASHINGTON TERRITORIAL LEGISLATURE IN 1854 WAS THE PARKER & COLTER STORE, SHOWN HERE CA. 1890. *Photo by W. A. Van Epps, WSHS, 1924.32.1*

During the early years, the Territorial Legislature met in less-than-ideal spaces. The first legislators assembled on February 28, 1854, in one of Olympia's largest buildings—the Parker & Colter Store near what is now State Avenue and Capitol Way. Its owner, Edmund Sylvester, added a second floor to accommodate the nine-member Territorial Council and the eighteen-member House of Representatives, which were made up of young men mostly representing western Washington Territory.

The first legislature created a territorial government framework, established new counties, designated a territorial seal, and authorized new roads—all in sixty-four days.

Although accommodations were rustic, local amenities helped popularize the town as the Territorial Capital—especially the Olympia oyster, called the "succulent lobbyist" by some for its popularity with the legislators who gathered in nearby hotels and eateries.

The second legislative assembly convened in late 1854 in the newly constructed Masonic Temple at what is now Eighth Avenue and Capitol Way and gave out territorial "prizes"—the university to Seattle and the penitentiary to Walla Walla. In 1855, the assembly designated Olympia as permanent Territorial Capital and petitioned the U.S. Congress for funds to erect a temporary capitol building.

Construction began on the Territorial Capitol in 1855 on the present Capitol grounds, but stalled when the Puget Sound Indian War of 1855–1856 drew away carpenters and builders. The third legislative assembly (1855–1856) convened again in the Masonic Temple. The fourth assembly (1856–1857) finally met in the new, wooden Capitol constructed at a cost of $5,000 and intended to be only temporary. It housed chambers for the Territorial Council and House of Representatives, as well as several committee rooms and a one-room public library—one

MASONIC TEMPLE AT 8TH AND CAPITOL IN OLYMPIA. LEGISLATIVE MEETING SITE, 1854–1855. *Photo by Asahel Curtis, State Library Photograph Collection, 1851–1990 (SLPC), WSA*

WINNING CAPITOL DESIGN BY ERNEST FLAGG, 1893, PUBLISHED IN *HARPER'S WEEKLY*. *Private Collection*

OPPOSITE: DELEGATES OF THE SECOND CONSTITUTIONAL CONVENTION AT THE TERRITORIAL CAPITOL, 1889. *Inauguration of Governor Ferry Photographs, 1889, WSA*

BREAKING GROUND FOR THE ANNEX TO THE OLD STATE CAPITOL BUILDING, 1901. GOVERNOR JOHN ROGERS IS IN THE FOREGROUND. *WSHS, C1958.181X.1*

of the first in the territory. The federal government later provided $30,000 for a permanent Territorial Capitol building, but squabbling over the capital's location kept the territory's lawmakers and governmental functions housed in the 1856 structure for more than four decades.

When Washington became a state in 1889, 132,000 acres of timberlands were set aside to finance construction of a permanent capitol. (The State still holds 109,400 acres of timberland in trust that benefit Capitol campus projects.) A State Capitol Commission was created in 1893 to guide the project. After a nationwide architectural competition that year, Ernest Flagg of New York City submitted the winning design, an "elegant and scholarly" single building with graceful dome and other classic architectural features. Excavation began at what was known as "Capitol Place," near the Territorial Capitol. However, political events and financial upheaval intervened and the foundation was the only progress made. As an interim solution in 1901, the State purchased the large and elaborate Thurston County Courthouse (now called the Old Capitol) for $350,000, expanding it for state governmental functions by 1905.

The original 1856 Capitol Building was torn down in 1911. The Parker & Colter building, later the Gold Bar Restaurant, became revered as a remnant of territorial Washington.

WASHINGTON LEGISLATURE IN THE OLD CAPITOL. *Photo by Walter P. Miller, University of Washington Special Collections (UWSC), UW11065, Social Issues Collections*

OLD CAPITOL IN OLYMPIA AFTER 1905. *Photo by C. D. Nichols, WSHS, 2006.156.8*

PRESIDENT THEODORE ROOSEVELT SPEAKING FROM THE OLD CAPITOL TO CROWDS IN CAPITOL PARK, MAY 22, 1903. *Courtesy of the Olympia Tumwater Foundation Archives*

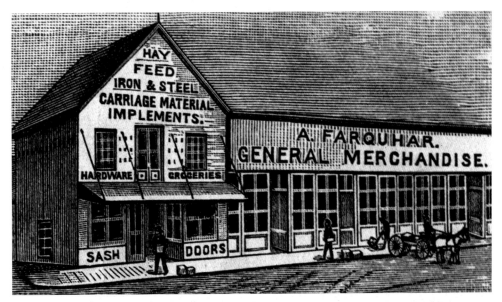

A. Farquhar, General Merchandise Building, 1901–1905. Legislative meeting site, 1903, near 7th and Adams. *Photo by Jeffers Studio, Susan Parish Photograph Collection, 1889-1990 (SPPC), WSA*

Opposite: Old State Capitol damage after the September 10, 1928 fire. *Photo by Vibert Jeffers, SPPC, WSA*

With preservation intentions, citizens moved the decrepit building, but it too was demolished by 1911. The Masonic Hall that had housed early territorial legislatures was torn down the same year.

The Old Capitol occupies a full block facing the town square (now Sylvester Park). The elaborate edifice, built of Chuckanut sandstone with round-arched openings and castle-like turrets, originally boasted a 150-foot-tall eight-faced clock tower. Designed by Willis A. Ritchie and built in 1891, it had proven too costly for the county.

Ritchie was commissioned to design an east wing for legislative chambers, this time in Tenino sandstone. However, the building was not complete for the 1903 legislative session. Instead, the legislature met in another downtown location, the Farquhar building, a barely adequate wooden structure dubbed "The Barn" by legislative pundits. Finally, lawmakers, state officers, executive departments, and administrative staff moved into the converted courthouse for the 1905 legislative session. At last, Washington's state government was centralized in a dignified building with modern amenities and room for all departments.

However, this facility soon became too cramped for the growing state's governmental functions and agencies. In 1911, the governor and legislature moved forward with efforts to again build a more spacious Capitol Building on Sylvester's donated acres. Within months of the legislators' departure in 1927, the Old Capitol suffered a disastrous fire which destroyed the clock tower. Repaired, the building continued as a facility for state agencies. It was again damaged by a 1949 earthquake and lost more of its signature turrets. The Old Capitol Building received a $9-million restoration in 1983 and now houses the Superintendent of Public Instruction, the primary agency charged with overseeing Washington's K-12 public education.

CHAPTER THREE

INTERVENING EVENTS

Remnants of the Flagg foundations, August 5, 1923. *SPPC, WSA*

Top: Perspective view drawing of the proposed State Capitol Group for the State of Washington in Olympia by Wilder and White architects, ink and pencil on board. *WSHS, C1963.50.21.3*

Nearly three decades (1893–1922) passed between the excavation of the foundation for architect Ernest Flagg's single-building design and the start of construction on the monumental Legislative Building that stands today. In the interim, the capitol project experienced several starts and stops.

A national depression in 1893 devastated the state's economy and the value of the timber trust stagnated. The legislators soon realized that Flagg's "one building for everything" plan was too small to accommodate Washington's expanding legislative and judicial functions. The Flagg plan was abandoned, and its foundation became a playground for local children. A seven-member Capitol Commission was organized in 1911 to move the project forward.

Another nationwide competition for the capitol design was launched, this time guided by the Washington Chapter of the American Institute of Architects (AIA). Thirty architectural firms submitted designs. A jury of three architects selected the Capitol Group plan and Temple of Justice design submitted by the Walter Robb Wilder and Harry Keith White firm from New York City.

The group plan was a new concept for American state capitols. Wilder and White's design was meant to be viewed from the north with the Temple of Justice and other buildings appearing as a base for the domed Legislative Building.

ARCHITECTS WILDER AND WHITE

HARRY K. WHITE. AFTER THE CAPITOL GROUP PROJECT, THE WILDER AND WHITE FIRM CONTINUED UNTIL 1930 AND WHITE LATER WORKED ON A VARIETY OF LARGE PROJECTS. HE DIED IN 1966. *DES*

WALTER R. WILDER. AFTER WILDER AND WHITE DISSOLVED IN 1930, WILDER SUFFERED FROM ILL HEALTH AND DIED IN 1934. *DES*

When in 1911 it was announced that the relatively unknown New York City firm of Wilder and White had won Washington State's competition for its new state capitol, it must have come as a surprise to the professional community, perhaps even to the winners, Walter Robb Wilder and Harry Keith White. The two partners were friends, having worked together as draftsmen for the well-known New York architectural firm of McKim, Mead, and White. Both had their educations at top-ranked schools, Wilder at Cornell University and White at the Massachusetts Institute of Technology. They had also had entered an earlier design competition, unsuccessfully, but good preparation for what lay ahead.

The two men worked harmoniously together. Wilder possibly was more the designer of the two, but evidence suggests that White in his managerial role was able to lure in more substantial clients. The dominant architectural flavor of their work was conservative—traditional and classical. Certainly that was standard practice of that time; the partners' education and their choice would have reinforced it. Known as the Beaux Arts method, it was rigidly ritualized and committed to classical architecture, formalism, and balance. Their competition submittal to Olympia reflects that bias.

Norman J. Johnston, Emeritus Professor of Architecture, College of Built Environments, University of Washington

Excavation work began in 1912 on the first building. The estimated value of the state's timber trust had reached $6 million by 1913. These funds, together with subsequent legislative appropriations, would finance the enormous construction project.

World War I stalled construction, as did disputes and disagreements about construction costs and the arrangement of the Capitol Group. Planning became a complicated political process, sometimes filled with controversy. The legislature, governors, and the State Capitol Commission wrangled over proper placement and orientation of the buildings. Alternate plans were proposed in 1912, 1915, and 1919. Nevertheless, the finished group would essentially reflect Wilder and White's 1911 architectural design.

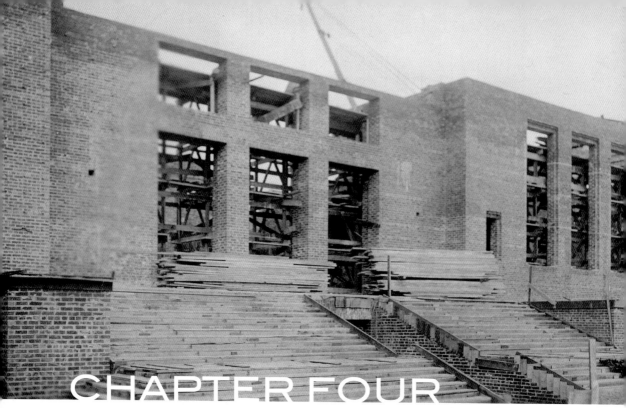

CHAPTER FOUR

CAPITOL GROUP—PLANNING, DESIGN, AND CONSTRUCTION

The mammoth effort to complete the Capitol Group unfolded over the course of nearly thirty years and brought to fruition the charm and dignity of Wilder and White's Capitol Group Plan, a harmonious ensemble of multiple masonry buildings surrounding the domed centerpiece, the Legislative Building. The American Neoclassical style of the Group incorporates architectural elements from Greek and Roman traditions—fitting for the "acropolis" of the classically named City of Olympia.

The first building to be completed, the Temple of Justice, set the tone for the design and style of all the other pieces. Begun in 1912, the building was completed in stages because of difficulties in financing. The Temple's raw brick walls remained uncovered until 1917, when it was faced with sandstone; it was not fully complete until 1920.

The Temple's exterior is Wilkeson sandstone, quarried in Pierce County about forty miles east of Olympia in the town of the same name. It is a durable stone favored for its warm off-white tones and hints of pink. The granite foundation is from Index in Snohomish County. All of the buildings in the Capitol Group feature at least some of these same exterior materials.

Approached by a broad flight of stairs from the south, the three-story building's temple-like front has a colonnade with eighteen simplified Doric columns under the wide fascia topped by a central, rectangular parapet. Side projecting elements each have two similar columns flanked by square pilasters supporting pediments.

Entered through massive bronze doors, the large foyer, stairways, and other public areas are faced with Alaska grey marble. The Temple has a gallery with pictures of all of the Territorial and State Supreme Court justices in the west hall on the main floor. The building currently houses the nine justices and their staff members as well as an extensive legal research library.

TEMPLE OF JUSTICE, 1930. *Photo by Merle Junk, SPPC, WSA*

ARCHITECT WALTER WILDER POSING ON THE TEMPLE OF JUSTICE, OCTOBER 5, 1918. *Harry White Photograph Collection (HWPC), PH 46.87, UWSC, UW21174*

OPPOSITE: WASHINGTON STATE TEMPLE OF JUSTICE CONSTRUCTION, FRONT VIEW, CA. 1916. *HWPC, PH Coll. 461.73, UWSC, UW29708z*

TEMPLE OF JUSTICE

Although the state's Capitol Commission planned to spend approximately $1 million to erect the Temple of Justice when it was approved in 1911, the initial contract only included a shell of a building without permanent flooring, doors, or door casings. The contract also failed to provide for the later added marble interior finish and sandstone veneer. Consequently, when the Supreme Court moved into this unfinished building in January 1913, it found that it had to carry on its business for several years amidst finishing work.

Although 2013 will mark the one-hundredth anniversary of the Supreme Court's occupancy of the Temple of Justice, the building is currently in as good a shape as it was when it was completed, despite the fact that over the years the building has been rattled by a number of earthquakes. The building's ability to withstand the massive Nisqually Earthquake of 2001 without structural damage was due in large part to earthquake-proofing that was done between 1987 and 1989.

Anyone entering the building today will quickly realize that it is an architectural gem. The beautiful entry foyer, magnificent courtroom, and stately main reading room of the State Law Library are the principal attractions on the main floor. These rooms, as well as the mezzanine above the foyer, and much of the lower floor are completely open and accessible to the public. Indeed, the court delights in welcoming the many visitors who enter the building each year.

Over the years a few people have advanced the notion that the architects erred in placing the Temple of Justice on the edge of the bluff. They suggest that the Legislative Building, commonly referred to as the Capitol Building, should have been placed on the view property. Most objective observers disagree, recognizing the brilliance of the architects' design, which placed the Legislative Building immediately south of the Temple of Justice, surrounded by the other buildings in the Capitol Group. Just as the architects envisioned long ago, this placement presents an appearance to observers in the city below that the Temple of Justice and Legislative Building are one building under a magnificent dome.

Although a few architectural features the architects envisioned for the Temple were not realized, such as statuary at the entrance and columns on the north side of the building, the building is admired as a great example of the Neoclassical style so prevalent in America's public buildings at that time. It has served our state well for nearly one hundred years.

Gerry L. Alexander, Justice, Washington State Supreme Court (Ret.), 1995–2011

ABOVE: VIEW OF THE TEMPLE OF JUSTICE LAW LIBRARY reading room. THE CAPITOL FURNISHINGS PRESERVATION COMMITTEE restored THE HISTORIC CORK-TOPPED TABLES IN THIS ROOM. *Washington State Senate (WSS)*

LEFT: TEMPLE OF JUSTICE, INTERIOR, 1920. *Photo by Joe Jeffers, SPPC, WSA*

The second structure of the Group was a general office building, designated as the Insurance Building in 1921. Also three stories in height, its architectural design and materials resemble the Temple of Justice, including the entrances which have colonnaded entries of Doric columns topped with a Greek pediment. Ornate bronze railings grace the north entry while the south entry features a steep set of steps. Begun in 1920 and completed in 1921, the building initially housed key state officers including governors Louis Hart and Roland E. Hartley. The interior has main hallways faced with Alaska grey marble, used in all the other Capitol Group buildings. Currently the building houses the insurance commissioner, the state auditor, and other executive staff offices.

After the cornerstone was laid in September 1922, construction began on the majestic centerpiece of the Group, the Legislative Building. The massive rectangular, four-level building rises the equivalent of twenty-two stories including the spectacular dome. The exterior walls of the building measure two and a half feet thick, including one foot of stone facing over brick.

Approached from the north, the main entrance is sheltered by a projecting portico consisting of eight Corinthian columns topped by carved acanthus leaves supporting a pediment with dentil details. Each of the ornate column capitals was carved in place by master stone carvers. All of the façades also have a colonnade of simplified Doric columns,

CONSTRUCTION PROGRESS ON THE INSURANCE BUILDING, WASHINGTON STATE CAPITOL COMPLEX, OLYMPIA, JULY 21, 1920. *Photo by Jeffers Studio, HWPC, PH Coll. 461.150, UWSC, UW26188z*

INSURANCE BUILDING, 1921. *SPPC, WSA*

GROUNDBREAKING CEREMONY FOR THE LEGISLATIVE BUILDING, 1922. *Photo by Jeffers Studio, HWPC, PH Coll. 461.187, UWSC, UW32257*

LEGISLATIVE BUILDING CONSTRUCTION, NOVEMBER 15, 1923, WITH THE FIRST ST. PETER HOSPITAL IN THE DISTANCE. *SLPC, WSA*

a unifying design element of the Group. The two wings contain the House Chamber on the west and the Senate Chamber on the east, each designed with vaulted glass roofs.

The crowning glory—the massive masonry dome—was the product of twentieth-century engineering innovations as well as architectural techniques used in the classical construction of European cathedrals. The 1,400 cut stones of the mammoth dome presented a challenge to stonecutters since none of the stones has a straight line on any edge or face. A specially designed cutter which cut stone from two sides was used. When the last stone was placed on October 13, 1926, exactly three-eighths of an inch projected on all sides, which was the exact specification in the architectural drawings!

Constructing the structure to support the dome required several continuous concrete pours. A mat of reinforced concrete, twenty-two feet thick and 130 square feet in size, supports four massive concrete piers, each nineteen feet square. These four footings rise eighty feet to the spring arches above. The entire weight of the masonry dome rests upon these arches and curved surfaces. The dome itself required 30.8 million pounds of masonry material—12.8 million pounds of stone and 18 million pounds of brick and concrete.

A cone-shaped structure of steel and concrete supports the outer dome, which was capped by a huge circular concrete slab upon which was placed the graceful stone cupola extending forty-seven feet high. A solid brick inner dome rests upon the interior row of twenty-four columns, forming the ceiling of the rotunda. The exterior colonnade supports the dome with thirty, twenty-foot-tall columns topped by Corinthian capitals. Each of these columns was carved on the ground then hoisted into place.

When completed, the Legislative Building contained more than 173 million pounds of stone, brick, concrete, and steel. Today, the 287-foot-tall structure remains one of the tallest self-supporting masonry domes in the world.

ARCHITECTURAL ELEMENTS

Architectural embellishments, both functional and beautiful, abound in the building. Wilkeson sandstone arrived at the construction site in a never-ending procession and master

LEGISLATIVE BUILDING CONSTRUCTION, OCTOBER 17, 1924. *SLPC, WSA*

LEGISLATIVE BUILDING CONSTRUCTION, MARCH 28, 1925. *SLPC, WSA*

Stone carvers, Legislative Building construction, 1920–1930. *SLPC, WSA*

"The outside work on the Capitol was mostly done by Scottish stonecutters. Many of them had worked together since their 'apprentice days' in the highlands of Scotland. My grandfather, Alexander Munro, was one of them. This picture was taken by my dad, who visited grandpa Munro on the jobsite in 1926. Our family has long been proud of this building and our family's involvement with it."—Ralph Munro, Secretary of State, 1980–2001.

Legislative Building construction. *SLPC, WSA*

LEGISLATIVE DOME CONSTRUCTION, 1926.
SLPC, WSA

TOPPING-OFF CEREMONY WITH GOVERNOR RO-
LAND HARTLEY ATOP THE DOME, OCTOBER 13,
1926. *SPPC, WSA*

UNLOADING COLUMNS FOR THE LEGISLATIVE
BUILDING. *Ralph Munro Collection*

stonecutters carved and shaped it. Like the other buildings in the Capitol Group, the foundation is faced with Index granite which is also used for the steps, platforms, sills, and doorways of the building. The simplified Doric columns in the colonnade around the building are four feet in diameter and twenty-five feet high with a slight taper at the top to assure visual harmony. The columns on the main north entrance and south portico are slightly larger, measuring thirty feet in height and four feet in diameter with their ornate Corinthian caps.

Noted architectural sculptor Maxfield H. Keck supplied plaster models for all ornamental stone, marble, and plasterwork in the building, such as the skull-and-wreath frieze harkening back to the state's pioneer heritage. Distinctive trim includes the *"cheneaux"* cornice and the egg-and-dart molding on the friezes. Keck's coffered ceiling designs on the portico and colonnades, as well as the interior halls, form exquisite geometrical patterns.

The 411-foot-long north terrace provides space for social events, political speeches, and other types of public gatherings. The terrace plinths have a carved fruit swag design surrounding the Washington state seal. Tiffany-designed bronze lanterns with antique glass line the balustrade.

WALKER CUT STONE COMPANY IN TACOMA CUTTING STONE FOR THE CAPITOL GROUP. *Marvin D. Boland Collection, BOLAND-B8354, Tacoma Public Library (TPL)*

LEGISLATIVE BUILDING, 1929–1931. *Photo by Vibert Jeffers, SPPC, WSA*

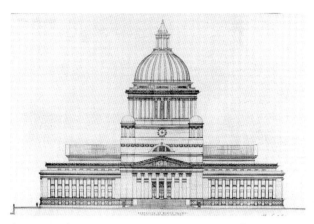

ARCHITECTS' NORTH ELEVATION DRAWING OF THE LEGISLATIVE BUILDING. *WSA*

CHIEF STONEMASON JOHN "MAC" MCIVER, THE CHIEF STONEMASON AT THE "TOPPING OUT" CEREMONY, OCTOBER 13, 1926. *HWPC, PH Coll. 461.314, UWSC, UW13182*

Forty-two steps lead up to the main north entry of the Legislative Building, commemorating Washington as the forty-second state to enter the United States. Flanked by monumental lanterns, the six bronze doors at the north main entry memorialize the pioneer era of the state, Washington's natural beauty, and its early industry. These themes were submitted from all over the state and interpreted by designer Maxfield Keck. The bronze doors were cast in New York and each door weighs two tons.

The ceiling of the main, north-facing entrance is adorned with rosettes, a classical motif seen elsewhere in the interior. On the building's south side, the open driveway is covered by a three-story *porte-cochère* (or portico) topped by a pediment. The columns here match those on the north side as do the sandstone rosettes overhead. Five sets of large, two-ton bronze doors exit to the *porte-cochère*, which is lit by a mammoth lantern.

GOVERNOR MON WALLGREN MAKES REMARKS AT THE CAPITOL AT HIS INAUGURATION ON JANUARY 10, 1945. *Richards Studio Collection, Series D18739-5, TPL*

When legislators marched from the Old Capitol in downtown Olympia to the completed Legislative Building on March 7, 1927, they entered a monumental building that still inspires awe today—a fitting venue symbolizing the Great State of Washington.

ADDITIONAL CAPITOL GROUP BUILDINGS

Development of the Capitol Group continued with the construction of two more buildings of the original Group Plan and additional structures.

Originally named the Highways Building, the Irving Newhouse Building was built in 1934 as a temporary six-month home for the Highway Department while the Transportation Building was under construction. Built in just over four months as a Works Progress Administration (WPA) project in a design by Olympia architect Joseph Wohleb, it was later used by the Department of Public Institutions and called the "Institutions Building." The two-and-one-half-story building is faced in pale brick with minimal sandstone architectural decoration, reflecting the spare modern design of the 1930s. Renamed in 1998,

THE SENATE CHAMBER WAS PACKED DURING A JOINT SESSION HELD ON MARCH 7, 1927. EARLIER IN THE DAY, THE LEGISLATORS HAD MARCHED FROM THE OLD CAPITOL TO THE NEW BUILDING. ALSO PRESENT WERE GOVERNOR ROLAND HARTLEY AND THE STATE SUPREME COURT. *Marvin D. Boland Collection, BOLAND-B16473, TPL*

LEFT: HUNGER MARCH, STATE CAPITOL, JANUARY 1933. *Photo by Merle Junk, SPPC, WSA*

RIGHT: EQUAL RIGHTS AMENDMENT RALLY, CA. 1972. WASHINGTON VOTERS PASSED AN EQUAL RIGHTS AMENDMENT TO THE WASHINGTON STATE CONSTITUTION IN 1972. *GSPC, WSA*

the building honors Irving R. Newhouse, a longtime legislator from eastern Washington, who served from 1967 to 1999. Although not part of the original Wilder and White plan, the building's entryway is faced with the Alaska grey marble featured in the other Group buildings. Today the building has Senate offices and serves other legislative functions.

Both of the diagonal-shaped Capitol Group buildings south of the Legislative Building were also designed by Joseph Wohleb using Wilder and White's Capitol Group design concepts to complete the buildings. Each building was constructed under Federal Emergency Relief Administration (FERA) programs of the Roosevelt Administration.

JOHN L. O'BRIEN BUILDING (TRANSPORTATION BUILDING), CAPITOL GROUP, STATE OF WASHINGTON, OLYMPIA. *Photo by Alfred G. Simmer, SPPC, WSA*

IRVING R. NEWHOUSE BUILDING (HIGHWAY BUILDING). *Photo by Vibert Jeffers, SLPC, WSA*

Differing from earlier Group buildings, both are constructed of reinforced concrete instead of brick and faced with Wilkeson sandstone. An underground tunnel joins the two buildings.

The John A. Cherberg Building (originally the Social Security and Public Lands Building) was completed in 1937. Renamed in 1985 for Cherberg, who served for thirty-two years as Washington's lieutenant governor from 1957 to 1989, the building was extensively renovated in 2006 and accommodates legislative hearing rooms as well as staff and Senate member offices.

The John L. O'Brien Building, originally the Transportation Building and later known as the Public Health and then House Office Building, was completed in 1940. Renamed in 1989, it honors twenty-six-term Seattle legislator and multi-term Speaker of the House John L. O'Brien, who retired in 1993. The building, rehabilitated in 2011, has House member and staff offices and legislative hearing rooms. Both buildings have ornate Art Deco bronze and stainless steel detailing in decorative finishes, fixtures, and carvings and main corridors lined with Alaska grey marble.

Unifying the buildings of the Capitol Group are the distinctive bronze lamps, each with balloon globes, that grace the front façades of the Newhouse, Cherberg, O'Brien, and Insurance buildings.

AERIAL VIEW OF THE CAPITOL GROUP, 1930–1934. *Photo by Merle Junk, GSPC, WSA*

JOHN A. CHERBERG BUILDING (SOCIAL SECURITY BUILDING). *Ellis Postcard, Private Collection*

PRITCHARD BUILDING, OLYMPIA, WASHINGTON. NORTHEAST APPROACH. *Photographer Shelley Metcalf, Washington State Library Special Collections (MS 321)*

The Joel M. Pritchard Building was constructed in 1959 to house the State Library. It was named in 1997 for Joel Pritchard, who served twenty-four years as a state legislator and congressman, and as lieutenant governor from 1989 to 1997, and was a champion for children's literacy.

Designed by internationally recognized Seattle architect Paul Thiry, it is considered to be one of the region's most important mid-century works of public architecture. It was among the first public structures to set aside a percentage of the total construction budget to purchase artwork for the building, and today the works of art commissioned for it are among the most valuable in the Capitol collection.

BUILDING FACTS

TEMPLE OF JUSTICE

1912–1920

Wilder and White Architects

270 feet by 125 feet

Construction $942,339.98

Furnishings $62,861.80

Total Cost $1,005,201.78

INSURANCE BUILDING

1920–1921

Wilder and White Architects

75 feet by 219 feet

Construction $1,032,035.00

Furnishings $51,462.97

Total Cost $1,083,497.97

LEGISLATIVE BUILDING

1922–1928

Wilder and White Architects

339 feet by 135 feet

Construction $6,795,595.88

Furnishings $594,172.33

Total Cost $7,385,768.21

Height of Dome 287 feet

IRVING NEWHOUSE BUILDING (FORMER HIGHWAYS BUILDING)

1934

Joseph Wohleb, Architect

70 feet by 125 feet

Construction $164,417.98

Furnishings $6,999.11

Total Cost $171,417.09

JOHN A. CHERBERG BUILDING (FORMER PUBLIC LANDS-SOCIAL SECURITY BUILDING)

1937

Joseph Wohleb, Architect, Wilder and White concept

83 feet by 235 feet

Construction $783,826.23

Furnishings $47,487.25

Total Cost $830,813.48

JOHN L. O'BRIEN BUILDING (FORMER TRANSPORTATION BUILDING)

1940

Joseph Wohleb, Architect, Wilder and White concept

83 feet by 235 feet

Construction $916,579.87

JOEL M. PRITCHARD BUILDING (FORMER STATE LIBRARY)

1959

Paul Thiry, Architect

200 feet by 100 feet

Construction $1,265,703.00

Art and Furnishings $34,297.00

Total Cost $1,300,000.00

CHAPTER FIVE

INSIDE THE LEGISLATIVE BUILDING

The Legislative Building's grand and stately exterior is befitting of the significance of the executive and lawmaking process of the forty-second state. No less impressive is the interior where the design for each room, corridor, rotunda, and stairway creates scenes of impressive splendor.

Entered from the ceremonial north-facing front façade of the building, the north vestibule introduces the exquisite finishes seen throughout the building—plasterwork of the vaulted ceilings and beautiful bronze grillwork along with monumental light fixtures.

Throughout the building are distinctive grey marbles—Tokeen, light grey in hue, and Gravina, a darker variety—both from Alaska quarries. The stones were all cut and polished in Tacoma, and along with other varieties they cost $850,000 when the building was built.

With an allocation of nearly $600,000, architects Wilder and White specially selected all of the designs for major furnishings for the building, including draperies and rugs supplied by Frederick and Nelson of Seattle and W. & J. Sloane and Company of New York. West-Made Desk Company of Seattle produced several hundred utilitarian furnishings, including oak desks, chairs, and bookcases used by accountants, secretaries, and stenographers. In the offices and other functional spaces, 54,000 square yards of plaster walls and ceilings were finished by C. H. Nelson, Master Plasterers of Seattle.

Offices for statewide elected officials are located in the four corners of the second floor. On the northeast corner, the Office of the Governor has oak, walnut, and mahogany furnishings crafted by W. & J. Sloane of New York. Portraits of governors holding office since the 1928 completion of the Legislative Building hang in the governor's office foyer.

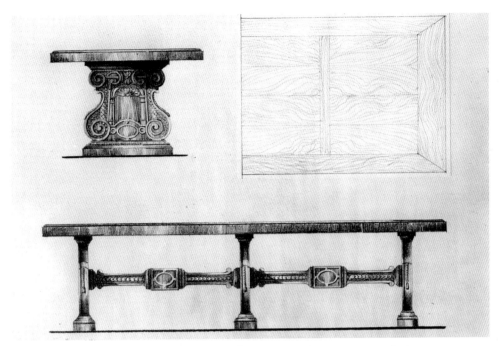

DRAWING OF TABLES FOR THE STATE RECEPTION ROOM. *Capitol Committee Records, WSA*

OPPOSITE: BRONZE DOORS, NORTH PORTICO. JAY JOHNSTON, AT LEFT, WAS THE ON-SITE REPRESENTA-TIVE FOR THE ARCHITECTS ON THE PROJECT. BEBB AND GOULD WERE THE LOCAL PARTNERS OF THE ARCHITECTS. PRATT AND WATSON OF TACOMA WERE THE FIRST PHASE CONTRACTORS AND SOUND CONSTRUCTION AND ENGINEERING COMPANY OF SEATTLE BUILT THE FINAL TWO PHASES OF THE LEGIS-LATIVE BUILDING. *WSHS, C1977.44.10*

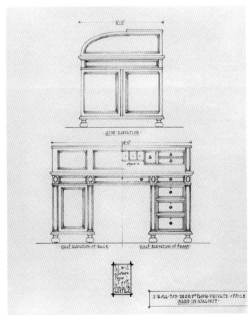

ROLL-TOP DESK. *Capitol Committee Records, WSA*

HOUSE AND SENATE PODIUM. *Capitol Committee Records, WSA*

The other executive offices have walnut appointments. Specially created leather chairs and sofas, hat racks, wastebaskets, and even 144 brass spittoons were part of the original décor. Throughout the building, fine-grain white oak was used for finish work.

The secretary of state, one of the original executive branch officers of both the state and territory of Washington, has executive offices in the northwest corner of the second floor of the building. The office lobby provides an opportunity to learn about Washington state history through temporary exhibits, literature, a replica of the state constitution, and a display case devoted to the symbols of Washington. A small store sells state seal items with the proceeds benefiting the work of the Capitol Furnishings Preservation Committee.

The office has most of the original historic furnishings and light fixtures. While the lobby has changed over the years, it maintains its 1928 appearance, welcoming people who come in to set up a corporation or charity, register for elected office, update their voter registration, obtain information about the State Library, or start their historic research with the State Archives.

Prior to the completion of the Capitol renovation in 2004, the Office of the Lieutenant Governor was located with other legislative leader offices on the third floor, but was reassigned to the historic location of the state auditor in the southeast corner on the second floor of the building. The state auditor is now housed in the nearby Insurance Building. The offices of the lieutenant governor feature historic furnishings from both the Legislative Building and the Old Capitol Building. The lieutenant governor's office has an original executive desk and roll-top desk in the space. The lobby has furniture previously used on the floor of the Senate Chamber in the Old Capitol Building including the president's rostrum from 1905, now the reception desk. Alongside the rostrum are the secretary's reading lectern and a member's floor desk, also from the old Senate Chamber. The Senate Rules Room, adjacent to the office foyer, has

GOVERNOR'S CONFERENCE ROOM, 1927. *SPPC, WSA*

SHOWN HERE IN THE GOVERNOR'S OFFICE, OFTEN THE SITE OF CEREMONIAL EVENTS, ARE LIEUTENANT GOVERNOR EMMETT T. ANDERSON ON THE FAR RIGHT WITH REPRESENTATIVES OF THE ANNUAL TOPPENISH POWWOW AND RODEO, CA. 1955. *SPPC, WSA*

OFFICE OF THE SECRETARY OF STATE FOYER, 2012. *Office of the Secretary of State*

OFFICE OF THE LIEUTENANT GOVERNOR FOYER. *Office of the Lieutenant Governor*

GOVERNOR'S VETERANS AFFAIRS ADVISORY COMMITTEE IN THE GOVERNOR'S CONFERENCE ROOM, 2012. THE CAPITOL FURNISHINGS PRESERVATION COMMITTEE RESTORED THE LARGE CONFERENCE TABLE AND SIDE TABLE. *Office of the Governor*

a number of high-back chairs original to the Legislative Building. Intended as seating for guests in the wings of the chamber, they are used here and on the Senate floor.

In this office, the Capitol Furnishings Preservation Committee installed a typical secretary's work station as it would have appeared in the building in the 1930s with a desk, wire recorder, intercom, telephone, and typewriter.

In the southwest corner of the second floor, the Office of the Treasurer displays an oak roll-top desk, one of forty-six ordered for use throughout the building in 1926. In another location for several years, the Capitol Furnishings Preservation Committee restored the desk and brought it home to the Legislative Building.

The treasurer's office has a working bank vault which is still in use today, although the locking mechanism has been modernized. The vault flooring, with a checkerboard pattern of brown and black squares, is one of the last remnants of the "rubber" floor tiles originally installed in many secondary corridors, storage rooms, and ground-level rooms.

On the east and west sides of this floor are the original Senate and House locker rooms with access to their respective chambers on the third floor. These rooms were members' lounges until the 1950s and later member cafeterias.

Impressive marble steps from the north and south formal entries lead to the mezzanine level of the rotunda. Here the interior dome rises 185 feet above the floor level where

Alaska Tokeen marble extends to the base of the dome with decorative plaster above. Politics and economy dictated that the dome would not have a marble interior. Twenty-four supporting columns are each twenty-five feet high and are made of steel with a plaster covering.

Although thirty murals were planned throughout the building and ideas for them have been presented several times, only the Senate and House chambers have had murals which are no longer in place. The current color décor was created in advance of the Washington State Centennial in 1989 to complement the historic plasterwork and marble.

On ledges at the four corners of the rotunda stand impressive light fixtures that are designed to resemble Roman firepots crafted in bronze and designed by the famous Tiffany Studios of New York. County flags for each of Washington's thirty-nine counties are on display behind the firepots, also a State Centennial project.

The building's magnificent lighting fixtures were all designed in bronze by the Tiffany Studios and are of myriad designs, incorporating many classical themes. The state paid $158,000 for all the pieces when they

ROTUNDA CHANDELIER, 2008. *DES*

ROTUNDA AND CHANDELIER. *WSS*

Rotunda view, 2008. *DES*

Chamber décor, 2008. *DES*

were installed. Dominating the central rotunda and suspended fifty feet above the floor, the mammoth Tiffany chandelier is eight feet in diameter, twenty-five feet high, weighs more than 10,000 pounds, and cost $10,000 when new.

The bronze state seal in the floor of the rotunda, originally designed by Olympia jeweler Charles Talcott in 1889 and interpreted here by Maxfield Keck, measures four feet in diameter and is wreathed by oak leaves and acorns to symbolize strength. For many years, the seal withstood foot traffic but the area is now protected by ropes after protests that George Washington's nose was being worn off. The fourth-floor bronze balconies repeat the state seal motif.

LEGISLATIVE CHAMBERS

The third floor houses the legislative chambers. Each chamber has a set of bronze central entry doors and the Senate Chamber still boasts an original set of leather-covered inner doors with bronze ornamental nails and small oval windows.

In the west wing, the House Chamber is lined with tan-colored Escalette marble from France, giving a warmer ambience than the Alaska grey marble in the public corridors.

The House of Representatives has ninety-eight walnut desks specially designed by the original architects, arranged in pairs on a carpet featuring the state flower, rhododendron, together with small trillium flowers.

The center aisle separates the two parties with the majority party on the north side. The Speaker of the House, the presiding officer, usually elected from the majority party, is chosen by all House members. During legislative sessions, the Speaker or Speaker pro tempore stands at the rostrum along with the Speaker's attorney. The chief clerk, deputy chief clerk, journal clerk, and reading clerk are seated before the Speaker. Above the ornately hand-carved rostrum is the electronic voting system that permits each member to vote from his or her desk for immediate tabulations reflected on the screen. The cabinet next to the rostrum is called "the cooler," where the House stores bills they may act upon in any particular session.

Added as part of the 1980s décor, both the House and Senate chambers have the names of the thirty-nine counties painted around the top frieze—in pairs, one each from eastern and western Washington—although Walla Walla County stands alone. The original plasterwork was also enhanced with color and gilding was added to the eagles and acanthus leaf decoration. The ceilings of both chambers offer exquisite designs and bronze grillwork that once allowed natural lighting in the chambers from skylights above, now closed over. Four magnificent bronze chandeliers frame each ceiling.

East of the rotunda, the Senate Chamber features a more dramatic Formosa marble from Germany with dark, reddish tones. A special technique of cutting marble is utilized on

ROMAN FIREPOT, ONE OF FOUR IN THE ROTUNDA, 2008. *DES*

STATE SEAL IN THE ROTUNDA. *WSS*

47

SENATE PAGES, 1943. LEGISLATIVE PAGES FORMERLY WORKED THE ENTIRE SESSION. NOW PAGES FROM ALL OVER THE STATE COME FOR ONE-WEEK STINTS TO LEARN THE LEGISLATIVE PROCESS. *Photo by Vibert Jeffers, SPPC, WSA*

the pillars here as well as in various other parts of the Legislative Building. "Book-matched" panels are produced when marble is sliced down the middle and opened up, producing a mirror image on each panel. The Senate carpet has a dogwood and rhododendron motif.

Seated at individual desks, the members of the majority party are at the north side of the center aisle and minority on the south side. The Senate votes by voice vote or oral roll call—a tradition that dates from the beginning of the Territory of Washington. Status boards and projected images display information about the proceedings.

During legislative sessions, the lieutenant governor presides in the Senate. When the lieutenant governor is absent from the rostrum, the president pro tempore takes the gavel. Seated beside the president at the upper desk are two Senate counsels who advise the presiding officer on parliamentary matters. Behind the front desk are the secretary of the Senate, who is the chief administrative officer, as well as the deputy secretary, the reading

STUDENT LEGISLATIVE DAY EVENT IN THE ROTUNDA, JANUARY 2011. *WSS*

clerk, and the journal and minute clerk. The sergeant at arms also occupies a seat on the rostrum. Separated from the floor by velvet curtains are the "wings" of both chambers which lead to leadership and administrative offices, caucus rooms, and in the Senate, lounges for members.

The operation of the legislature has changed over the years. One of the time-honored traditions was to stop or remove the clock or even put a drape over it at the end of the allotted time to pretend that the session was not over, allowing the legislature to work extra hours or days to complete its work. The State Supreme Court ended the practice in 1973. Today, special legislative sessions are called when legislators need more time to complete their work.

From 1927 to 1965, the legislature was housed almost entirely on the third and fourth floors of the Legislative Building and members' desks on the floor served as their offices. Large committee hearings were held in the chambers and those testifying were at the rostrum. Now the O'Brien, Cherberg, Newhouse, and Legislative buildings have member offices and hearing rooms.

The way in which bills are prepared for legislative action has also changed. The Bill Rooms were for many years in offices just off the floors of both chambers. Bills were hand-entered by typists for copying and clerks worked overnight to fill members' bill books for the next day's session. Later, the Bill Room (now called the Legislative Information Center) moved to the first floor, where it is today. Although some bills are still printed upon request, legislators (and members of the public) now access them online from the legislative website.

The third-floor north rotunda corridor between the House and Senate chambers was long known as "Ulcer Gulch," where lobbyists or the "Third House" traditionally held forth. Before the advent of cell phones, phone booths were located here and sometimes

House of Representatives Chamber. *WSHOR*

Senate Chamber, 2009. *WSS*

hundreds of lobbyists congregated as they monitored the progress, if any, of bills—a process so stressful and hectic that it often gave them ulcers! Today, lobbyists continue to influence and inform legislators using electronic messaging as well as passing notes or "working the doors" to give the members information during session.

STATE RECEPTION ROOM

The entry to the "Parlor of Washington"—the State Reception Room on the south side of the third floor—is highlighted by a Belgian marble entryway. Here, the elegance and majesty of the entire building come into focus. The Bresche Violetta marble from Brescia, Italy, is dramatic in its fanciful markings—a rabbit, butterfly, and even a profile of George Washington can be discerned with a little imagination. Likewise, the columns display

SENATOR PAULL SHIN AND STUDENTS FROM SEAVIEW ELEMENTARY SCHOOL IN THE SENATE CHAMBER, 2005. *WSS*

HOUSE BILL ROOM, 1963. *SPPC, WSA*

THE TOTAL EXPERIENCE GOSPEL CHOIR PERFORMS IN THE HOUSE CHAMBER IN CELEBRATION OF MARTIN LUTHER KING DAY, 2007. *WSHOR*

the unusual veining in the marble. The plasterwork here is also monumental. The ceiling's molded octagonal coffers hold the familiar rosettes displayed throughout the building bordered by an ornate cornice design. During the 2004 renovation of the building, the skylight over the room was uncovered to allow natural light to again flood the interior.

The waterfall chandeliers, with over 10,000 Czechoslovakian crystal beads each, weigh about one ton. The room also has complementary wall sconces of equal beauty.

The French velvet drapery, from the Frederick and Nelson store in Seattle, has the state seal hand-stitched using twenty-four-carat gold thread, the only gold used in the building. Marble plaques above the draperies feature gargoyles and mythological figures. The fireplaces at either end of the room, with their ornate bronze and-irons, were designed to burn coal but have been closed off. The carpet specially woven for the room covers a herringbone-pattern teak floor. Measuring over twenty-five feet by fifty-five feet, it was the largest single-loom rug in the world when it was made by the Mohawk Company of New York. During inaugural balls in the building, the rug is rolled up for dancing.

All of the furniture was designed for the room and the seven-foot round center table is especially striking with its top of inlaid wood and intricate carved base of solid Russian Circassian and walnut wood. W. & J. Sloane of New York supplied the furnishings including the chairs, originally covered with tapestry which featured Martha Washington in her garden.

A ceremonial flag for the state, donated by the Washington State Daughters of the American Revolution (DAR) in 1929, is displayed in the room. The more familiar green and gold state flag was officially adopted on June 7, 1923.

CUSPIDOR CARAVAN

Governor Roland Hartley took office in 1925, bringing with him suspicions about the Legislative Building project. Often at odds with the other two members of the Capitol Committee—C. W. Clausen, state auditor, and Clark V. Savidge, lands commissioner—Hartley was especially unhappy about the cost of furnishings for the building. Instead of awarding contracts to the "lowest bidder," as Hartley suggested, they were purchased using the architects' specifications for quality.

In 1928, the governor decided to take his issues on the road in the "Hartley Cuspidor Caravan." He loaded up furniture from the Capitol and traveled the state complaining about the profligacy of government. He presented as evidence one of the sixty-seven-pound brass cuspidors designed for the rotunda purchased at a cost of one hundred dollars.

During his successful 1928 re-election campaign, Hartley continued railing against the architects with complaints about the furnishings, flooring, and landscaping of the Capitol Group, although Hartley was the first Washington governor in the new Legislative Building and its ornate governor's office.

Governor Roland Hartley with Legislative Building furnishings. *Photo by Vibert Jeffers, Photograph Collection 1889–1990, WSA*

RECEPTION ROOM, 2008. *DES*

THE 2009 INAUGURAL BALL, SHOWN IN THE STATE RECEPTION ROOM. *WSS*

OPPOSITE: ROTUNDA VIEW, 2008. *DES*

Above the west fireplace hangs a forty-two-star U.S. flag, a remnant of celebrations sur-rounding Washington achieving statehood as the forty-second state in the Union. The Reception Room has hosted presidents and kings but citizens and schoolchildren visit the room as part of the guided tours of the building.

The fourth floor, accessible by side stairways or elevator, houses various legislative of-fices. Visitors can access the House and Senate public galleries by north and south doors where they can watch floor action during sessions from the original benches designed for the building. The ground level of the building with the signature marble hallways has various offices, a cafeteria, and meeting rooms as well as the Columbia Room, situated directly beneath the rotunda.

The magnificent Legislative Building, with its unequaled finishes and furnishings, is an important legacy for all Washingtonians to enjoy and protect.

CHAPTER SIX

THE CAPITOL GROUNDS

Located on a crest overlooking Puget Sound, the Capitol campus is a showplace of Washington with beautiful plantings, monuments, and fine architecture. Listed on the National Register of Historic Places, the west campus encompasses fifty-one acres and the entire campus is approximately 225 acres.

At the north end of the west campus are the General Administration Building built in 1956 and the Capitol Greenhouse built in 1939.

Topping the hill to the west of the Legislative Building is the Governor's Mansion. Built in 1908, it is the oldest building on the campus. Constructed for the governor to host visiting dignitaries during the Seattle Alaska-Yukon-Pacific Exposition of 1909, it was envisioned as a temporary structure. The Georgian red brick building was designed by Tacoma architects Russell and Babcock. Preserved through the efforts of then first lady Nancy Evans and The Governor's Mansion Foundation in the early 1970s, the house boasts one of the best collections of American furniture in the United States, including some original Duncan Phyfe pieces. Renovated and enlarged in 1974 and restored after the 2001 Nisqually Earthquake, the mansion is open weekly for tours by the Governor's Mansion Foundation.

ABOVE: GOVERNOR'S MANSION, 1968. *Photo by Werner Lenggenhager, SLPC, WSA*

OLMSTED LEGACY

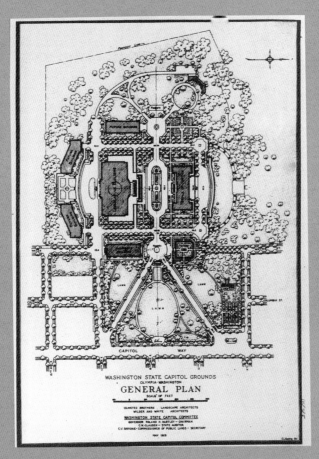

OLMSTED DESIGN FOR THE CAPITOL CAMPUS. *WSA*

The Washington State Capitol campus has one of the most extensive and intact Olmsted-designed capitol landscapes in the nation. Credited with having established the practice of landscape architecture in the United States at the turn of the twentieth century, the Olmsted Brothers created many of the nation's finest master-planned parks and wove public greenways into the fabric of city and community designs across the nation. In all, they designed eleven capitols, including the U.S. Capitol. They began work in the Pacific Northwest in 1903.

After an initial consultation in 1911, the Olmsteds were hired by the State Capitol Committee to design the grounds in 1927, and created one of the most prominent Olmsted landscapes in Washington State. The grounds reflect the firm's signature design approach that incorporates the unique and defining qualities of the natural environment, rather than creating a space apart from its setting. Here in Olympia, the rich natural setting includes views northward of the Cascade and Olympic mountains, views east to Mount Rainier, an encircling swath of forested hills to the south and west, and the meandering Deschutes River below the bluff on which the campus is set.

The Olmsteds designed these capitol grounds in a way that draws on the strength of these defining natural assets, but they also created intimate and formal landscaped spaces around and amid the classical buildings. Visitors experience a progression of increasingly formal spaces as they move toward the public courtyard at the heart of the campus, between the Legislative and Supreme Court buildings. In doing so, they created a metaphor for the democratic process, in which diffuse ideas are gradually refined into formal laws.

Capitol grounds landscaping, digging, 1930. *Photo by Vibert Jeffers, SPPC, WSA*

Washington State celebrated its one-hundredth birthday in 1989. Pictured is the kick-off event at the Capitol on November 11, 1988, to inaugurate the centennial year. Over 800 volunteers, coordinated by the Department of Natural Resources, formed an outline of the state and the number "100" with umbrellas. *WSHS, 2012.3.2.11*

HONORED IN THE LEGISLATIVE BUILDING

The two statues in the north foyer of the Legislative Building honor Mother Joseph of the Sisters of Charity of Providence (Esther Pariseau) and Marcus Whitman, an early physician and missionary, who are Washington's representatives in the National Statuary Hall Collection in the U.S. Capitol. Others honored on the third floor are civil rights leader Martin Luther King, Jr. and George Washington.

MOTHER JOSEPH STATUE, 2008. *DES*

MARCUS WHITMAN STATUE, 2008. *DES*

LEFT: GEORGE WASHINGTON BUST, SCULPTED BY DR. AVARD FAIRBANKS AND DONATED TO THE STATE BY THE MOTHER JOSEPH FOUNDATION. *DES*

RIGHT: MARTIN LUTHER KING, JR. BRONZE BUST BY JEFF DAY. DEDICATED IN 1986 BY THE STATE MLK HOLIDAY COMMISSION. *DES*

Time capsule burial, November 11, 1953. Governor Arthur Langlie is in the center. *WSHS, C2012.1.2.35.2*

Tivoli Fountain dedication, 1953. Peter G. Schmidt representing the Olympia Tumwater Foundation, the donor of the fountain, at the dedication, April 15, 1953. *Photo by Merle Junk, SPPC, WSA*

MARKING TIME AT THE CAPITOL

A sense of history pervades the Capitol grounds and time capsules have been a way to mark special events in Washington and national history.

In the center floor of the north vestibule of the Legislative Building, a marble tile marks the time capsule placed during the U.S. Bicentennial by then Governor Dan Evans in 1976. Inside are seeds, quilts, photographs, Native American art, maps, preserved salmon, an Olympia Beer can, and a model of a spacecraft. The capsule is scheduled to be opened in the year 2076.

The State Centennial Time Capsule in the center door entry of the south portico is an updatable time capsule. Dedicated on Centennial Day, November 11, 1989, by the Washington Centennial Commission, the capsule is meant to be "interactive" with new deposits every twenty-five years until the final unveiling in 2389.

The Washington Territorial Time Capsule was buried in the Flag Circle near the base of the center pole in 1953 to be opened in 2053. Oddly, a second time capsule "Territorial Time Capsule II," now located nearby, was discovered during the Capitol renovation that followed the 2001 Nisqually Earthquake. The first capsule was buried as intended, but the other was lost and eventually listed as one of the ten most sought-after time capsules

Z. A. VANE IS SHOWN STANDING IN FRONT OF THE "WINGED VICTORY" MEMORIAL ON THE CAPITOL CAMPUS, JUNE 20, 1938. *SPPC, WSA*

in the world. Forty-nine years later, a cleaning crew preparing for repairs to the Legislative Building discovered a wooden crate hidden against a wall. The crate might have been thrown away if the work crew hadn't noticed the handwritten words "time capsule" on its side. It now rests alongside its mate, awaiting the 2053 opening.

MEMORIALS

Several memorials complement the buildings of the Capitol Group on the west campus. A plaque, installed by the Sacajawea Chapter of the Daughters of the American Revolution (DAR) in 1928, on the southeast corner of the Legislative Building, marks the approximate location of the Territorial Capitol. Two other DAR plaques identify the massive George Washington Elm scion tree north of the Legislative Building and the site of the Governor Isaac and Margaret Hazard Stevens House near 11th and Capitol Way. Several other memorial plantings are also on the campus.

VIETNAM VETERANS MEMORIAL DEDICATION, MAY 25, 1987. *WSS*

FIREWORKS OVER THE CAPITOL. *WSHOR*

The bronze World War I memorial, "Winged Victory," was designed by sculptor Victor Alonzo Lewis in 1938 and restored in 2008. Three larger-than-life servicemen and a Red Cross nurse are depicted under the outstretched arm of the goddess Nike, standing twelve feet high. Near the memorial is the state Medal of Honor obelisk, dedicated in 1976, a replica of the one in Medal of Honor Grove in Valley Forge, Pennsylvania.

The first Vietnam War memorial, just to the west of the obelisk, was installed in 1982 and later refitted in 1988 to honor Washington prisoners of war and those missing in action. Constructed through private donations, a second Vietnam Veterans Memorial, east of the Insurance Building, was dedicated on May 25, 1987. The names of the 1,123 Washingtonians killed or missing in the war are etched into the green, polished granite monument that can be touched and seen by all.

The World War II Memorial dedicated in 1999 on the north part of the campus honors nearly 6,000 Washington residents who gave their lives in battle. The memorial features large bronze blades, 4,000 metal wheat stalks, and engraved granite pavers. A monument honoring Korean War veterans is on the East Capitol campus.

Dedicated in 2006 and located near the Temple of Justice, the Washington State Law Enforcement Memorial honors law enforcement officers in Washington killed in the line of duty.

Longtime legislator and legislative historian Sid Snyder, who began working in Legislative Building in 1949 and retired in 2002 from a career in the House and Senate, was honored in 2006 when a portion of 14th Avenue SE was renamed "Sid Snyder Memorial Avenue" in his honor.

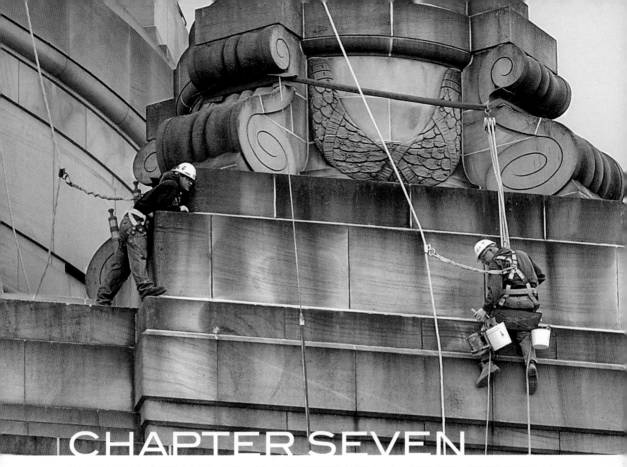

CHAPTER SEVEN

EARTHQUAKES AND REPAIRS, PRESERVATION AND CONSERVATION

The glorious domed Legislative Building "built to last the ages" was challenged little more than twenty years after its completion. On April 13, 1949, the strongest earthquake in the state's recorded history jolted western Washington, measuring 7.1 on the Richter scale. Surprisingly, the major damage from the quake was limited to the cupola atop the Legislative Building. The 180-ton stone cupola was replaced for a cost of $155,000 with a lighter, 110-ton steel structure resembling the original. The cupola lantern was relit using solar power in 2004.

On April 29, 1965, another major earthquake shook western Washington, registering a magnitude of 6.5 and damaging the dome. To increase its strength, the dome was reinforced with a sixty-foot-high, one-foot-thick treatment of sprayed-on concrete. The building's three sections were bound together more securely by steel and concrete rein-forcements.

In 1971, more structural reinforcements lent strength to the Legislative Building. Brick interior walls received a thick layer of reinforced concrete and the porches, rotunda, and flanking wings were bolted together. By 1976, $9.6 million had been spent repairing the domed building and preparing it for the next quake. The test would come twenty-five years later.

On February 28, 2001, the Nisqually Earthquake centered near Olympia rattled the Capitol campus and the rest of western Washington. The forty-five-second quake mea-suring a 6.8 magnitude damaged the upper colonnade near the rim of the dome, shifted sandstone blocks, and knocked exterior columns askew. The four Roman firepots located in the rotunda—each weighing 3,000 pounds—moved sideways. Emergency repairs cost more than $1 million, and the building was vacated for nearly four months.

ABOVE: WORKERS CHECKING THE CONSOLES, 2003. *DES*

DAMAGE FROM THE 1949 EARTHQUAKE. *Photo by Merle Junk, SPPC, WSA*

WORKERS REPAIRING MORTAR ON THE LEGISLATIVE BUILDING, 2003. *DES*

A major renovation in 2002–2004 involved $6.5 million in seismic work including fastening elements together and strengthening the columns surrounding the dome. Other work in the $101-million project included safety upgrades and renewing infrastructure for twenty-first-century use, as well as carving replacements for some stones damaged on the lantern in the 1949 earthquake. The building emptied for the work and re-opened in January for the 2005 legislative session.

A MESSAGE FROM THE LIEUTENANT GOVERNOR

As the president of the Senate, I often encourage new senators to take time from their busy schedules to appreciate the majesty of the building in which we have the privilege to work. The details of our State Capitol building are magnificent, from the beautiful Tiffany chandelier in the rotunda to the names of each of the thirty-nine counties painted along the ceilings of the chambers.

The Legislative Building and the entire Capitol campus exemplify the magnitude of the responsibility with which we are entrusted, to serve the people of our state. The people of Washington have given us this environment in which to serve. It is monumental and significant. Our service to the people of Washington must be equally monumental and significant; these buildings are a daily reminder that we owe them nothing less. Every day I walk in, I am inspired to do the work of the people who have sent us here to represent them.

Office of the Lieutenant Governor

Brad Owen
Lieutenant Governor of Washington
1997–Present

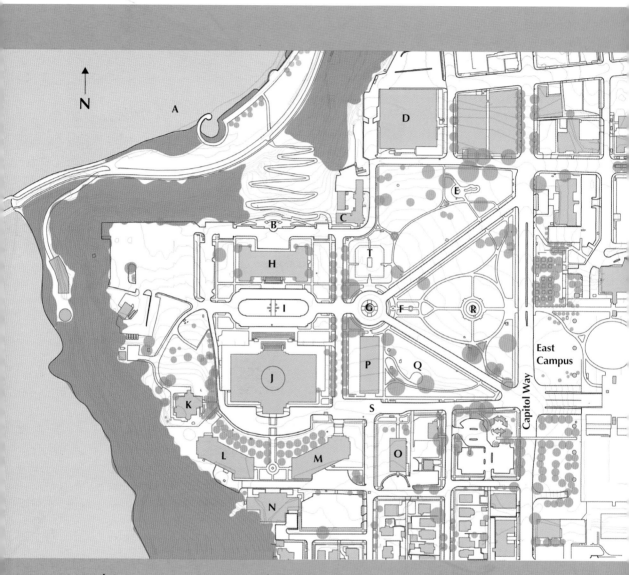

Washington State Capitol Campus

A. Capitol Lake

B. Law Enforcement Memorial

C. Greenhouse

D. General Administration Building

E. World War II Memorial

F. Medal of Honor and POW/MIA Memorials

G. "Winged Victory" World War I Memorial

H. Temple of Justice

I. Flag Oval (time capsule)

J. Legislative Building

K. Governor's Mansion

L. John L. O'Brien Building

M. John A. Cherberg Building

N. Joel M. Pritchard Library

O. Irving Newhouse Building

P. Insurance Building

Q. Washington State Vietnam Veterans Memorial

R. Tivoli Fountain

S. Sid Snyder Memorial Avenue

T. Sunken Garden